THE BOOK OF DANIEL

Rose Visual Bible Studies

The Book of Daniel
Rose Visual Bible Studies

Published by Rose Publishing
An imprint of Tyndale House Ministries
Carol Stream, Illinois
rose-publishing.com

ISBN 979-8-4005-0496-9

Author: Titus O'Bryant, ThM, Senior Pastor, LifePoint Church, Reisterstown, MD

Printed in China
31 30 29 28 27 26
8 7 6 5 4 3 2

Contents

The God of heaven will set up a kingdom that will never be destroyed, nor will it be left to another people. It will crush all those kingdoms and bring them to an end, but it will itself endure forever.

Daniel 2:44

The Book of Daniel

Have you ever been far from home and felt the sharp pangs of homesickness? An old American folk song, first recorded by Dick Burnett in 1913, captures that lonesome, troubled feeling of being far from home. This song has been altered many times by various artists and is thought to have originated in Ireland more than two hundred years ago. One well-known version begins like this:

> I am a man of constant sorrow,
>   I have seen trouble all my days.
> I bid farewell to ol' Kentucky,
>   the place where I was born'd and raised.
> For six long years I've been in trouble,
>   my pleasure here on Earth is done.
> For in this world I have to ramble,
>   I have no friends to help me now.

The biblical prophet Daniel found himself carried away far from home with no prospects of ever seeing his homeland again. He could have written the words to that old folk song, bidding farewell to ol' Jerusalem and finding trouble for sixty-five long years. As a teenager, he was taken to Babylon as a political prisoner. He was pledged in service to the king who had devastated his homeland. His captors changed his name and tried to assimilate him into their way of life.

The book of the Bible that bears Daniel's name records several events from his life, along with messages about the future. The book is concerned with two main questions:

- How can believers in God live faithfully and effectively as exiles far from home?
- In a world that seems chaotic with rising and falling kingdoms, how is God still the sovereign king over all?

Daniel's book moves between these two questions, as it flows from telling the story of Daniel and his colleagues in Babylon to recording Daniel's prophetic visions and interpretations of the world's kingdoms and God's eternal kingdom.

By studying the twelve chapters of Daniel's writings, you can come away with a stronger faith in the God who oversees all human history to accomplish his purposes but who is also intimately connected with the events of our individual lives.

1 FAR FROM HOME

Daniel 1

Far from Home

When you're far from home, feelings of loneliness and longing for family and all that is familiar are very common. Daniel must've felt that way—and intensely so. He was a teenager when Babylonian forces invaded his homeland of Judah. His nation suffered a humiliating defeat, and he was taken nearly a thousand miles away to serve his conquerors. Young Daniel didn't know it then, but he would spend the rest of his life, about sixty-five years, in Babylon.

How could Daniel survive (and even thrive) in a land that didn't share his religion or respect his values and yet still maintain his faithfulness to God? The first test that Daniel and his fellow captives—Shadrach, Meshach, and Abednego—faced was one concerning food and drink. They were told to consume the food and wine from the king's table, but for Daniel and his friends, doing this would have been "defiling" (Dan. 1:8). How Daniel handles this challenge in chapter one gives us insight into the kind of man he was and would continue to be as he faced even greater tests of integrity later in life.

Read It

Key Bible Passage

Read Daniel 1, which gives background information about the setting for the book of Daniel and introduces us to Daniel and his companions.

Optional Reading

Read 2 Chronicles 36:1–21, which describes Nebuchadnezzar's invasion of Jerusalem and the fall of Judah.

Daniel was determined not to defile himself by eating the food and wine given to them by the king.

DANIEL 1:8 NLT

Know It

1. What are God's actions and the gifts he gives in Daniel 1:2, 9, 17?

   ❏ verse 2:

   ❏ verse 9:

   ❏ verse 17:

2. Do these gifts surprise you? What does this tell you about God's relationship with us and the events in our world?

3. Why do you think Daniel and his friends refused the king's food and wine? What might have been defiling about it?

Explore It

Timeline of Daniel

BABYLONIAN EMPIRE

Chapter 1
Daniel trained in Babylon

605 BC
Nebuchadnezzar invades Jerusalem. Daniel is taken captive to Babylon.

Chapter 2
Nebuchadnezzar's statue
(2nd year of Nebuchadnezzar)

586 BC
Nebuchadnezzar destroys Jerusalem and the temple and sends the people into exile.

Chapter 3
Shadrach, Meshach, and Abednego in the fiery furnace*

Chapter 4
Nebuchadnezzar's fall and restoration*

562 BC
The Babylonian Empire is in turmoil after the death of Nebuchadnezzar.

Chapter 7
Vision of the four beasts
(1st year of Belshazzar)

553 BC
Belshazzar governs Babylonia as coregent with his father, Nabonidus.

Chapter 8
Vision of the ram and goat
(3rd year of Belshazzar)

Chapter 5
Belshazzar's feast and the writing on the wall
(last year of Belshazzar)

539 BC
Babylon falls to the Medo-Persian Empire.

MEDO-PERSIAN EMPIRE

Chapter 9
Daniel's prayer
(1st year of Darius the Mede)

538 BC
Cyrus the Great of Persia permits exiles to return home. Jews begin returning to Jerusalem.

Chapter 6
Daniel in the lions' den*

536 BC
Jerusalem temple rebuilding begins.

Chapters 10–12
Daniel's final vision and probable date of death
(3rd year of Cyrus)

*Date unknown

The Last Kings of Judah

During the volatile time period spanning from the fall of Assyria to the rise of Babylon, the final kings of Judah struggled to maintain their throne. Josiah reigned as Judah's sixteenth king from about 640 to 609 BC. He is best known for removing polytheistic practices from worship in Jerusalem and throughout the kingdom and returning to the worship of Yahweh, the one true God (2 Kings 22–23; 2 Chron. 34–35). Josiah's reforms followed many years of entrenched idol worship.

For about twenty years, the Babylonians and the Medes (from the kingdom of Media) joined forces in attacking the Assyrians, until finally breaking Assyrian dominance. Around 609 BC, an Egyptian army intending to aid the last of the Assyrians in Carchemish marched through Judah. King Josiah attempted to block Egypt but was defeated and died in the battle.

Josiah's successor lasted only three months. Then came King Jehoiakim who suffered defeat by Nebuchadnezzar in 605 BC and only retained his throne by pledging loyalty to Babylon. (Daniel and his friends were taken to Babylon as captives around this time.) Jehoiakim's son, Jehoiachin, succeeded his father in 597 BC during a time of unrest. Judah had chosen to rebel against Babylon and faced swift retribution. Nebuchadnezzar's armies defeated Judah again, and Jehoiachin was taken to Babylon after reigning only three months.

Nebuchadnezzar selected another of Josiah's sons, Zedekiah, to be the next king in Jerusalem. His reign lasted about eleven years, until he also chose to revolt against Babylon. This time Nebuchadnezzar showed no mercy. In 586 BC, he ended Judah's ability to defend itself by tearing down their fortresses. He attacked their identity and religious life by destroying their temple. He burned their capital city of Jerusalem to the ground. He brutalized the people and exiled most of them to Babylonian territories. Zedekiah was forced to watch the execution of his children before being blinded and taken as a prisoner to Babylon (2 Kings 25; 2 Chron. 36:11–19).

Many of the people in Judah had led quiet lives of faithfulness to God, yet they still experienced the terrible consequences of their faithless and unwise leaders. Sometimes we, too, can get caught in the backwash of God's judgment falling on others and experience painful consequences. The decisions others make can have a real impact on our lives. Yet we are called to faithfulness, whether we are experiencing the best in life or the worst.

The Flight of the Prisoners
(James Tissot, c. 1896–1902)

In the book of Daniel, we find accounts of how Daniel and his friends were rescued from seemingly certain death—more than once. (Though of course they still had to endure the trauma of being thrown into a furnace or a den of lions!) Many believers throughout history have also faced the prospect of death because of their faith, but not all were rescued from martyrdom. Consider how this New Testament perspective on the reality and expectation of persecution can help us cope with suffering:

> Now we call him, "Abba, Father." For his Spirit joins with our spirit to affirm that we are God's children. And since we are his children, we are his heirs. In fact, together with Christ we are heirs of God's glory. But if we are to share his glory, we must also share his suffering. (Rom. 8:15–17 NLT)

> We must certainly distinguish between what God would like to see happen and what he actually does will to happen, and both of these things can be spoken of as God's will.
>
> **I. Howard Marshall,** in *The Grace of God, The Will of Man*

Zedekiah's Cave

Near the Damascus Gate of Old City Jerusalem is a natural entrance to a cave. This cave opens beneath the Old City and runs under the modern-day Muslim Quarter of the city. After passing through its entrance, visitors come upon a large cavern more than 300 feet (91 m) wide. Out of this large space, one can follow paths chiseled into the rock to explore galleries and caverns that circle back around to the same opening.

This large area is an ancient quarry. Josephus called it the Royal Caverns. Some people believe that Solomon had stones for his temple construction cut from this quarry. Herod the Great used this area as a quarry for his renovation of the temple. The stones that still stand in the Western Wall today are quite likely from this quarry.

According to one legend, Zedekiah, the last king of Judah, tried to escape from Babylonian soldiers through the tunnels of the quarry. A large deer running nearby attracted the attention of soldiers who followed the deer to the entrance of the cave, where Zedekiah emerged and was captured. The water that drips through the ceiling of the cavern is nicknamed Zedekiah's tears.

New Names in Babylon

In Daniel 1:7, the chief official gives Daniel and his friends new Babylonian names—one of several ways to try to strip them of their Judean identity and assimilate them into their new culture.

HEBREW NAME	MEANING	BABYLONIAN NAME	MEANING
Daniel	God is my judge	Belteshazzar	Bel, protect his life
Hananiah	Yahweh is gracious	Shadrach	Command of Aku
Mishael	Who is what God is?	Meshach	Who is what Aku is?
Azariah	Yahweh will help	Abednego	Servant of Nego [Nebo]

Bel, Aku, and Nebo are names of Babylonian gods.

When Was Daniel Written?

Traditionally, Daniel is regarded as the author of his book. However, some modern commentators argue that the book was written around 165 BC, during the tumultuous reign of Antiochus IV who attacked Jerusalem and desecrated the temple. They contend that Daniel was not a historical figure who lived during the times of Nebuchadnezzar and Cyrus in the sixth century BC, but instead a later author in the second century BC told a story about a character named Daniel and set it in an earlier time to encourage faithfulness to God during a season of adversity. Part of the motivation for this argument seems to be that it explains how the detailed prophecies in chapters 7–12 concerning Alexander, the Greek Empire, and the competing Greek kingdoms that followed Alexander's death in the fourth century BC could be possible; the prophet Daniel, after all, according to the book, lived two centuries before Alexander.

The book of Daniel itself repeatedly provides specific information about when events occurred:

- Daniel's story begins during "the third year of the reign of Jehoiakim king of Judah" when "Nebuchadnezzar king of Babylon came to Jerusalem and besieged it" (Dan. 1:1). These events took place in 605 BC.
- The final verse of chapter 1 states that "Daniel remained there until the first year of King Cyrus" (Dan. 1:21). Cyrus overcame Babylon and began his reign in 539 BC.
- Throughout the book, Daniel includes other references, but chapter 1 clearly makes the claim that his career extended from Nebuchadnezzar's siege of Jerusalem until the victory of Cyrus over the Babylonians, an impressive career in public service for more than sixty-five years—and an even more impressive life of faithfulness.

As people of faith, we have no reason to doubt that God could work through Daniel to predict the future; so it seems best to take Daniel at face value and accept the date of his writing and ministry as he reports it.

How Was Daniel Written?

How the book was written is also interesting. The book is unusual because it was composed using two different languages. Chapter 1 is in Hebrew, while chapters 2–7 are in Aramaic, before returning to Hebrew for chapters 8–12.

Why would Daniel have composed his book in this way? Perhaps it was because chapters 2–7 present a cohesive unit about the kingdoms of the earth turning beastly and chapters 2 and 7 are closely connected because they essentially repeat the same predictions about rising and falling kingdoms. These predictions can also help us understand the remaining prophetic sections of the book (chapters 8–12) that describe cycles of behavior leading to the end of time when God establishes his kingdom.

Another way to look at the structure of Daniel is as two parts: chapters 1–6 contain narratives about select events, and chapters 7–12 are the prophetic visions given to Daniel.

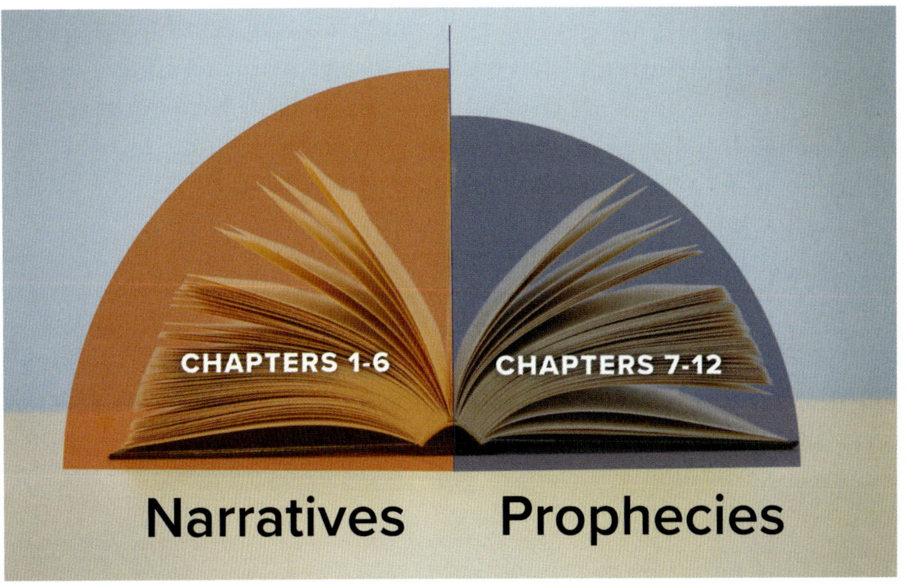

Integrity

One characteristic that sets Daniel apart from the crowd is his integrity. Integrity means living a consistent life where what others see on the outside matches the character on the inside. It means living a life true to the values and beliefs that a person professes. Integrity is a quality that anyone can work to develop regardless of age, experience, or even past failures.

In engineering, structural integrity refers to the ability of a building or some other type of structure to bear its own weight, while resisting becoming bent or deformed, and to safely maintain its intended purpose and design. That's not a bad definition for what integrity looks like in the life of a believer. As our life is designed around the principles and qualities found in the Bible, through our obedience, we are able to carry our own weight in life and find the strength to bear up under pressure to complete God's intended purpose for us.

That's the kind of example we find in Daniel. He did what was right when he was carried away to Babylon. We don't know exactly why consuming the king's food and drink would've broken a boundary for Daniel. It may have been because it was offered to idols before being served to the king's household or because the food didn't meet Jewish dietary restrictions. Whatever the reason, the food from the king failed to meet the standards that God had called to Daniel to observe. At a time when no one would have chided Daniel for assimilating into Babylonian culture, he chose to live with integrity. Integrity requires doing what is right when no one is watching, when no one cares what you do, and also when others are watching and the stakes are high.

Here's one final thought about integrity: It's never too late to build a life of integrity. Near where I live, a bridge is undergoing repairs. Because of its age, it had to be stripped to its foundations and rebuilt. Even when we've failed, it's possible to begin again. When we submit ourselves to the Lord and obey his word, we may be stripped down to our foundations, but we can rebuild again—even after a failure.

Life Application Questions

1. Describe a time when you felt the weight and pressure of expectations or demands that went against your values. How did you respond?

2. What are you tempted to consume that could be "defiling" (Dan. 1:8), and how can you avoid those temptations?

3. Do you think that God's sovereign control over everything eliminates the possibility of events taking place that God does not wish to happen? Why or why not?

4. Daniel and his friends continued trusting God, even when life was difficult and painful. Is your faith conditional on God doing what you think he should do? How can you know?

5. Think about an experience or season of life in which you faced adversity. How did it affect your faith in God?

6. Daniel and his friends needed one another during their exile. Is there someone you could encourage right now, or is this a time when you need some encouragement from a friend?

Notes

Daniel 2–3

Prospering in Babylon

Have you ever had the chance to observe a tree growing out of a rock? Some trees have adapted to obtain nourishment from the rock's minerals. Others take root in a small amount of soil and then push through the rock, creating a break in the rock. There's something beautiful and captivating about seeing a living thing flourish in an environment where you think it doesn't belong.

Daniel and his friends likely felt that they didn't belong in Babylon. Ripped away from their homeland and family, they must have grasped for ways to put their roots down and remain grounded. And they did. They found ways to live faithfully to their God while also serving the people of Babylon and the king.

These young men are examples to us of how to walk the tightrope of living in the world but not belonging to it (John 17:15–16). Like them, we can learn how to flourish in our Babylons.

Read It

Key Bible Passage

Read Daniel 2. In this chapter, King Nebuchadnezzar threatens Daniel and all of Babylon's "wise men" with death; Daniel receives knowledge and the meaning of Nebuchadnezzar's strange dream; and Daniel provides the dream and its interpretation to the king and is promoted to a high leadership position.

Also read Daniel 3, in which Shadrach, Meshach, and Abednego stand against Nebuchadnezzar's demands to worship his idol and are thrown into a furnace—but rescued by God.

Optional Reading

Read Jeremiah 29:1–23, which includes the prophet Jeremiah's letter to exiles.

> The rock that struck the statue became a huge mountain and filled the whole earth.
>
> DANIEL 2:35

Know It

1. How did Daniel handle Nebuchadnezzar's unreasonable request and the threat against his life and the lives of his colleagues?

2. Pay close attention to Daniel's prayer in 2:20–23. Consider this prayer against the backdrop of Daniel's defeated nation, his captivity and forced service in Babylon, and the urgent threat against his life. What does Daniel praise God for?

3. As you read Daniel 3, imagine you are a bystander observing the events. Use your five senses to experience the story.

   - ❑ What do you see?
   - ❑ What do you hear?
   - ❑ What do you feel?
   - ❑ What do you taste?
   - ❑ What do you smell?

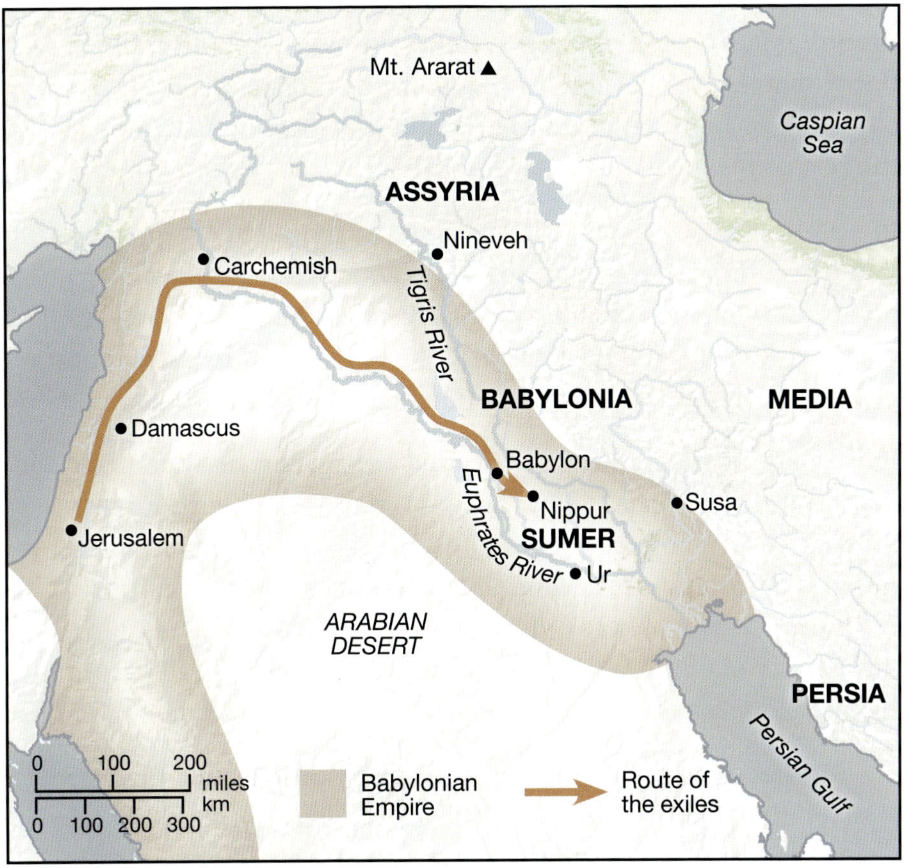

Nebuchadnezzar and the Neo-Babylonian Empire

The history of the Babylonians extends to the brink of recorded human history. During the Bronze Age (3300–1200 BC), the Babylonians were a Sumerian people group rising from just northwest of the Persian Gulf between the Tigris and Euphrates rivers. They were often called Amorites or Chaldeans, and they formed an early civilization based in city-states. These "Old Babylonians" helped develop cultures throughout the ancient Near East.

After a lengthy conflict with the Hittites, Babylon endured more than a century under Assyrian rule. Nabopolassar, the founder of the Neo-Babylonian Empire, seems to have been a general or military leader overseeing the southern region of the Assyrian Empire. He engaged in a rebellion against Assyria and rallied the Babylonians. He was able to establish the independence of the city-state of Babylon in 626 BC, and he fought the Assyrians for the rest of his life.

In 605 BC, Nabopolassar died during his son Nebuchadnezzar's military campaign abroad, causing Nebuchadnezzar to make a remarkably fast journey back to Babylon to be crowned king, before returning to the battlefield. (It was around this time that Daniel and others in Judah were taken to Babylon.)

In 601 BC, Nebuchadnezzar invaded Egypt, but he was never able to fully conquer Egypt. Twice, Judah joined with Egypt to rebel against Nebuchadnezzar, and twice was defeated. Each setback became more severe, until 586 BC when the temple in Jerusalem was destroyed, the city burned, and the people mercilessly slaughtered. Jeremiah provides some details around Nebuchadnezzar's conquest and the fall of Jerusalem:

> On the tenth day of the fifth month, in the nineteenth year of Nebuchadnezzar king of Babylon, Nebuzaradan commander of the imperial guard, who served the king of Babylon, came to Jerusalem. He set fire to the temple of the LORD, the royal palace and all the houses of Jerusalem. Every important building he burned down. The whole Babylonian army, under the commander of the imperial guard, broke down all the walls around Jerusalem. (Jer. 52:12–14; see also Jer. 38–39; 2 Kings 25)

The Neo-Babylonian Empire is regarded as one of the greatest in history, although it lasted less than a century. They quickly accumulated incredible wealth and power. Nebuchadnezzar expanded the power of Babylon from the Persian Gulf to Asia Minor (modern-day Turkey) and to the borders of Egypt, including modern-day northwestern Saudi Arabia and the land of Israel. He rebuilt the city of Babylon and created the famous Hanging Gardens, one of the Seven Wonders of the Ancient World. Nebuchadnezzar's forty-three-year reign set a mark for the aspirations of later rulers, and his building projects made Babylon the center of the world.

The Hanging Gardens of Babylon,
(Charles Mills Sheldon, 1924)

The King's Wise Men

"One night ... Nebuchadnezzar had such disturbing dreams that he couldn't sleep. He called in his magicians, enchanters, sorcerers, and astrologers, and he demanded that they tell him what he had dreamed" (Dan. 2:1–2 NLT).

The king's advisers had received training for about three years to enter specific roles:

- Magicians were dream interpreters. This was an established role in Egypt and Mesopotamia. They kept journals of images in dreams with keys to understanding those images.
- Enchanters were believed to have skills in defending against harmful omens and dreams.
- Sorcerers were people who cast spells.
- Astrologers were royal advisors who counseled kings on matters of state, economics, and the supernatural. The word for astrologer is often translated as "Chaldean." Chaldeans were originally an ethnic group closely related to Babylonians, but over time the groups merged into one, and this term came to identify various "wise men."

Nebuchadnezzar believed that he was a special instrument for the gods on earth and that the gods would communicate their intentions and will to him through dreams. His request was so outlandish ("First, tell me my dream and then its meaning") that it's possible Nebuchadnezzar had trouble remembering his own dream. Forgetting a dream was thought to be an especially bad omen, because it meant that the gods were causing confusion and hiding their plans from the king.

Sometimes, unscrupulous advisers used their special "abilities" to unduly influence or usurp a king by making dire predictions to manipulate the king. Perhaps Nebuchadnezzar was paranoid about palace intrigue or attempts to overthrow him and wanted to keep his advisers off-balance by not telling them what the dream was.

In the dream, Nebuchadnezzar saw a large statue of a man made of different materials: gold, silver, bronze, iron, and clay. The dream also included a rock cut from a large mountain that crushed the statue to bits. The statue was blown away without a trace. The rock then grew to cover the entire earth.

Daniel did what all the other wise men couldn't: He described the dream and revealed its meaning. The statue represented five kingdoms that would succeed one another and present different qualities. By viewing history through the lens of Daniel's interpretation, we can observe several successive empires.

Head of Gold
Babylonian Empire

Chest and Arms of Silver
Medo-Persian Empire

Belly and Thighs of Bronze
Greek Empire

Legs of Iron and Feet of Iron and Clay
Roman Empire and the mix of world powers that followed

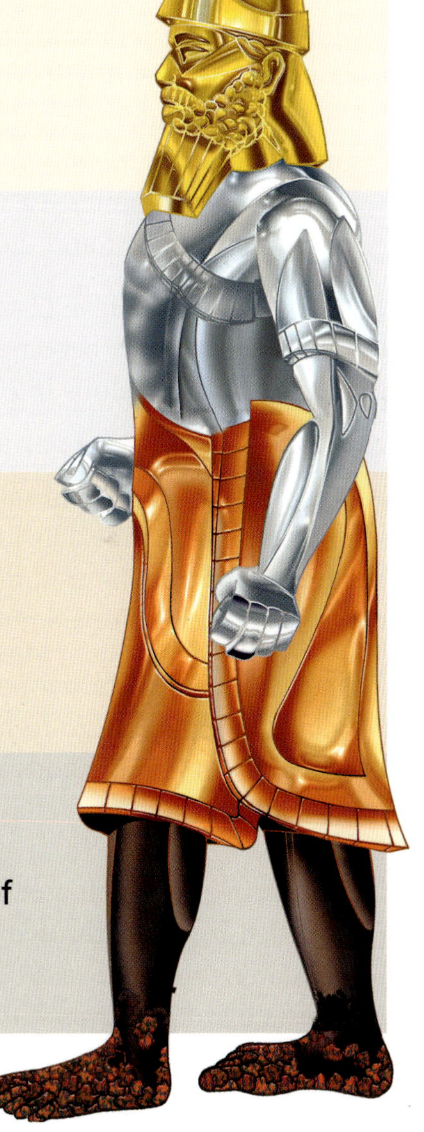

Our Eternal Kingdom

In Daniel's interpretation, the most important feature is not the rising and falling kingdoms of the earth but the kingdom that overtakes them all and lasts forever:

> In the time of those kings, the God of heaven will set up a kingdom that will never be destroyed, nor will it be left to another people. It will crush all those kingdoms and bring them to an end, but it will itself endure forever. This is the meaning of the vision of the rock cut out of a mountain, but not by human hands—a rock that broke the iron, the bronze, the clay, the silver and the gold to pieces. (Dan. 2:44–45)

Jesus quoted Psalm 118:22–23 when he declared, "The stone the builders rejected has become the cornerstone. The Lord has done this, and it is marvelous in our eyes"(Mark 12:10–11).

While all the powers of this earth struggle for dominance and its kingdoms blink into obscurity, God is building his kingdom without human hands. His kingdom has been operating in the background throughout human history and will one day cover the entire earth in his glory.

Perhaps it was this eternal perspective that motivated Shadrach, Meshach, and Abednego to be so resolute in refusing to bow down and worship the gods and kings of this earth. Daniel's friends knew who the everlasting King of Kings was, and they knew he was "mighty to save" (Isa. 63:1). They declared, "King Nebuchadnezzar, we do not need to defend ourselves before you in this matter. If we are thrown into the blazing furnace, the God we serve is able to deliver us from it, and he will deliver us from Your Majesty's hand. But even if he does not, we want you to know, Your Majesty, that we will not serve your gods or worship the image of gold you have set up" (Dan. 3:16–18).

Life Application Questions

1. Besides Daniel and his friends, what other examples from the Bible can you think of in which painful or challenging events are redeemed by God as a witness for him?

2. How might Daniel's three friends have felt about being promoted to serve the king after he attempted to kill them (Dan. 3:30)? When have you experienced conflicting feelings about your calling or what you believe God is asking of you?

3. Read Daniel 3:25. Is there a situation in your life where you can trust God to be present with you "in the fire"? What does it mean for you to be confident about his presence with you at *all* times?

4. What fiery furnaces have you experienced or are in now? What might change if you understood those experiences as refining you to make you stronger, rather than judging you for not being good enough?

5. Take a moment to reflect on the sovereignty of God, the reality of his eternal kingdom, and your current responsibilities in life. How can you be faithful ...

- ❑ as a citizen?
- ❑ in your church?
- ❑ to your family?
- ❑ in your career?
- ❑ with your gifts and opportunities?
- ❑ as a child of God?

6. Make a list of three painful or challenging parts of your life story. Ask God to redeem those events to somehow work for your good and for his glory. Can you see him already at work in those areas?

Notes

Daniel 4–5

God Reigns Over All

In chapters 4 and 5, the character of proud and foolish kings is set in contrast to the humble and wise character of Daniel.

- After falling into madness, King Nebuchadnezzar realizes that God reigns over all kings (chapter 4).
- With the fall of Babylon and the death of King Belshazzar, it's clear that God is the judge who calls all to give account of themselves (chapter 5).

In both stories, God show that his reign and authority extend over all earthly rulers.

We only have a few snapshots in the Bible from Daniel's long life. In fact, about twenty to thirty years pass between chapter 4 and chapter 5. Though we don't know what happened to Daniel during those decades, we can see from his interactions with Belshazzar that the prophet's life and message still demonstrate the same consistent faithfulness to God that he showed when he was a young man in Nebuchadnezzar's court.

Read It

Key Bible Passage

Read Daniel 4, which details another dream from Nebuchadnezzar and interpretation from Daniel, along with the fascinating way God humbled the king.

Read Daniel 5, which shows the arrogance of the Babylonian rulers continuing to unfold while the faithfulness of Daniel keeps pointing to the sovereignty of God over all.

Optional Reading

Read Jeremiah 50, which is God's word through Jeremiah about the destruction of Babylon because of the nation's arrogance and wicked deeds.

The Most High God is sovereign over all kingdoms on earth and sets over them anyone he wishes.

DANIEL 5:21

Know It

1. What do you observe about the character of each man from the stories in chapters 4 and 5?

   - ❏ Nebuchadnezzar:

   - ❏ Belshazzar:

   - ❏ Daniel:

2. What actions does Belshazzar take that demonstrate his arrogance?

3. How does the reign of God compare with the authority of Nebuchadnezzar and Belshazzar—and even of rulers today?

Belshazzar of Babylon

Following Nebuchadnezzar's reign, which ended in 562 BC, the reigns of a series of Babylonian kings were cut short by palace intrigue and assassinations. The final ruler of the Neo-Babylonian Empire was Nabonidus, who had killed the previous ruler to take the throne. Nabonidus worshiped a moon god and spent much of his reign in a northern Arabian city connected with that system of worship. Absent from the city of Babylon for most of his reign, Nabonidus established his son, Belshazzar, as coregent in Babylon.

Though Daniel 5 refers to Nebuchadnezzar as Belshazzar's "father," this term likely meant "predecessor," a common usage in the ancient Near East. It's also possible that "Nebuchadnezzar" became a title used by later kings or that the name became misspelled as the name Nabonidus. In a language without vowels this would have meant changing NBKD (Nebuchadnezzar) to NBNY (Nabonidus).

In Daniel 5:16, Belshazzar offers Daniel the opportunity to become the third highest ruler in Babylon for revealing the strange writing on the wall. This was, in fact, the highest position Belshazzar could offer. Belshazzar was himself in the second highest position because his father was the actual king, though much responsibility had been given to Belshazzar.

Belshazzar died in the fall of Babylon to the Medes and Persians in 539 BC (Dan. 5:30), but his father, Nabonidus (who had returned to the city), survived, though he was sent away to live in exile.

The Writing on the Wall

In chapter 5, Belshazzar and his guests are frightened by mysterious words written on the wall during their raucous party. The words are so shrouded in mystery that Daniel is called out of retirement to reveal their meaning.

Even after the interpretation in verses 26–28 and centuries of study, the meaning of the writing on the wall retains some of its mystery. *Mene, Mene, Tekel, Parsin* are the words God sent to Belshazzar as a prediction of judgment and the end of his reign and life. Hebrew and Aramaic scholars suggest that these words have to do with weights and measurements.

- *Mene* corresponds to *mina*, and *tekel* to *shekel*. These words refer to weights used for measuring grain, oil, and precious metals.
- *Parsin* seems to indicate half or being divided into half.

More than likely, it wasn't the words themselves that confused Belshazzar, but the significance behind the words. Daniel explained how Belshazzar had been measured, weighed, and found wanting. He would face the judgment of his kingdom being divided up by his enemies; in other words, for Belshazzar it was "the writing was on the wall."

Those who have trusted Jesus need not live in fear of judgment, because "there is now no condemnation for those who are in Christ Jesus" (Rom. 8:1). But those who have rejected Jesus will face judgment. As the apostle John wrote, "I saw the dead, great and small, standing before the throne, and books were opened. Another book was opened, which is the book of life. The dead were judged according to what they had done as recorded in the books" (Rev. 20:12). Believers will still be accountable to God and receive rewards based on their faithfulness in following Jesus, and they will answer to the Lord for their lives: "'As surely as I live,' says the Lord, 'every knee will bow before me; every tongue will acknowledge God.' So then, each of us will give an account of ourselves to God" (Rom. 14:11–12).

Belshazzar, motivated by foolish pride, had brought to the banquet cups and bowls designed to measure and weigh substances for worshiping the Lord in his temple and used them for drunkenness and praising pagan gods (Dan. 5:4). Ironically, Belshazzar himself was *measured* by the Lord and judged. Each of us would be wise to remember that we will personally give account to God for our stewardship of the life he has entrusted to us.

Belshazzar's Feast (Rembrandt, 1636)

Three Prophets of the Exile

Although God's people were experiencing judgment because of their long-term rebellion, God's presence was with them in exile. He called them to repentance through the prophets Jeremiah, Daniel, and Ezekiel. These three prophets overlapped in their ministry but had different settings and influences.

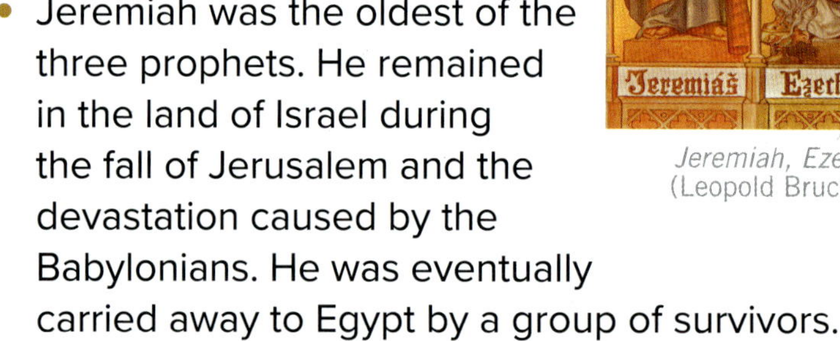

Jeremiah, Ezekiel, Daniel
(Leopold Bruckner, 1905)

- Jeremiah was the oldest of the three prophets. He remained in the land of Israel during the fall of Jerusalem and the devastation caused by the Babylonians. He was eventually carried away to Egypt by a group of survivors.

- Ezekiel was born to become a priest but was taken into exile during the second wave of captives from Jerusalem, around 597 BC, a few years after Daniel was taken. Ezekiel lived and prophesied outside the city of Babylon with other exiles, probably in a settlement by Nippur for workers who maintained canals and waterways for the province of Babylon.

- Daniel enjoyed the longest life of these three prophets and rose to great political influence in Babylon. He witnessed the first Babylonian invasion of Jerusalem and later the fall of Babylon to Persia. Daniel lived just long enough to see his exiled people begin to return to their homeland.

Waiting for Our King

In the world and in our lives, Jesus is king right now. Yet there are still many rulers and authorities in this present world that claim power over us: governments, businesses, sickness, and even death. Although Jesus is *already* king, we do *not yet* experience the full benefits of his kingdom authority.

So we wait. We wait for our king to take his throne and subjugate all other powers beneath him. While rulers and empires come and go, the great mountain of the kingdom of God has been growing and will crush every other power beneath the one who holds all power and authority.

> The Kingdom of God is the redemptive reign of God dynamically active to establish his rule among men.... This Kingdom, which will appear as an apocalyptic act at the end of the age, has already come into human history in the person and mission of Jesus to overcome evil, to deliver men from its power, and to bring them into the blessing of God's reign. The Kingdom of God involves two great moments: fulfillment within history (already), and consummation at the end of history (not yet).
>
> **George Eldon Ladd**, *The Presence of the Future*

Life Application Questions

1. What evidence do you see in this world that Jesus is *already* the king who reigns over all?

2. What evidence do you see in this world that the fullness of Jesus's reign is *not yet*?

3. Are you humble like Daniel or arrogant like Belshazzar? Do you ...

   - ❑ listen before speaking?
   - ❑ feel entitled to the best of everything?
   - ❑ lose patience when your intentions are frustrated?
   - ❑ maintain a balanced perspective whether you are promoted or overlooked?
   - ❑ speak confidently without manipulation?
   - ❑ make unreasonable demands and take advantage of others?
   - ❑ look for praise from people around you?

4. What are some factors in your life that make it tempting to forget that God rules over all things?

5. How can you reorder your life to recognize that God is your king?

6. Read Galatians 5:22–23. Consider how trusting that God is in control contributes to the fruit which the Holy Spirit develops in you.

- ❏ Love:
- ❏ Joy:
- ❏ Peace:
- ❏ Patience:
- ❏ Kindness:
- ❏ Goodness:
- ❏ Faithfulness:
- ❏ Gentleness:
- ❏ Self-control:

Notes

Daniel 6

Blessings in Disguise

Have you ever heard the old tale about a farmer and his son? It's a wisdom story from Chinese culture about blessings in disguise.

A farmer and his son had a magnificent and much-loved horse who helped the family earn their living by farming. One day, the horse disappeared; it had run away. The neighbors all commiserated with the farmer, "Your horse ran away—what terrible luck!" The farmer responded, "Maybe so, maybe not."

A few days later, the great horse returned home, leading a string of wild horses behind him. The neighbors shouted, "Your horse came back and brought wild horses home—what great luck!" The farmer replied again, "Maybe so, maybe not."

Later that week, the farmer's son was trying to tame one of the wild horses, and he was thrown to the ground, breaking his leg. The neighbors cried out, "Your son broke his leg—what terrible luck!" The farmer again responded, "Maybe so, maybe not."

A few weeks later, soldiers from the national army marched through town, recruiting all the boys for the army. They did not take the farmer's son because he had a broken leg. The neighbors all thought, "We've got him now." They shouted, "What tremendous luck—your boy was spared!" To which the farmer stubbornly replied, "Maybe so, maybe not. We'll see."

Sometimes blessings arrive in unexpected packaging, and what seems harmful turns out to be helpful. In Daniel 6, we see Daniel once again demonstrating his faithfulness and strong character, even when it put his life at risk. As a result of his steadfast determination to worship and talk with the Lord, the authorities fed him to lions! But what appeared to be quite terrible turned out to be a miraculous blessing.

Read It

Key Bible Passage

Read Daniel 6, a story of Daniel's faithfulness to God in the face of danger, and God's faithfulness to Daniel to save him.

Optional Reading

Read Ezra 1:1–11, which is King Cyrus's decree allowing the exiles to return to Jerusalem.

[Daniel] went home to his upstairs room where the windows opened toward Jerusalem. Three times a day he got down on his knees and prayed, giving thanks to his God, just as he had done before.

DANIEL 6:10

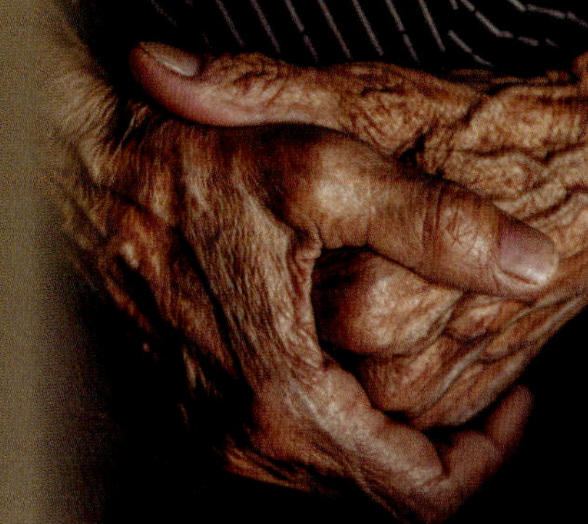

Know It

1. What motivated Daniel's enemies to craft a plot to bring him down?

2. Imagine you are with Daniel when he learns about the king's decree. How do you respond?

   Imagine you are in the room with Daniel when he prays with the windows open. What will you do?

   Imagine you are watching as Daniel enters the lions' den. What do you see, hear, smell, and feel?

3. As a result of the plot against Daniel, what happened to each of the characters at the end of the story?

   - ❑ Daniel:
   - ❑ The conspirators:
   - ❑ The king:
   - ❑ The people of the kingdom:

Explore It

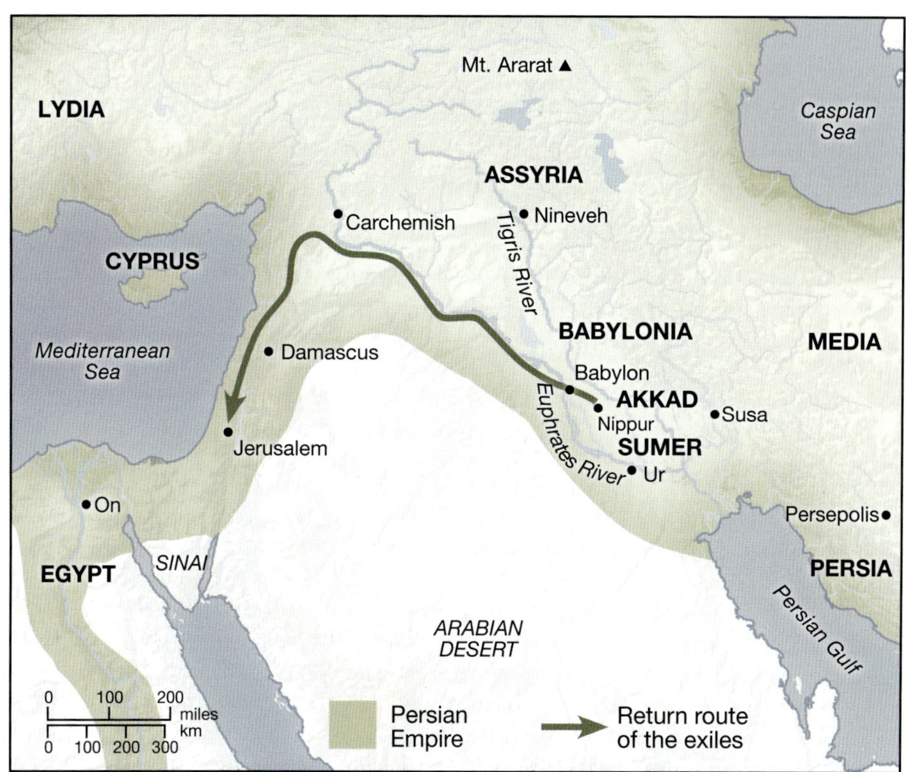

Cyrus the Great and the Persian Empire

For over two hundred years, the great power on earth was the Persian Empire. Eventually, their rulers called themselves "the kings of kings."

The character of the Persian Empire was inseparable from the identity of Cyrus II, who reigned from 559 to 530 BC. His grandfather, Cyrus I, had married his son, Cambyses, to Mandane, daughter of the king of the Medes, in an attempt to unite the kingdoms of Media and Persia. Cambyses and Mandane had a son whom they named Cyrus II, but he would be remembered as Cyrus the Great.

After ascending to the Persian throne upon his father's death, Cyrus and his maternal grandfather, the king of the Medes, entered open conflict. A significant faction from the Median army revolted and joined Cyrus, who defeated the armies of his grandfather and united the Medes and Persians into one empire.

Following this victory, he marched west to invade the wealthy kingdom of Lydia. The king of Lydia was Croesus, who is thought to have been the first ruler to mint gold as currency, contributing to the ancient phrase "rich as Croesus." This victory brought Cyrus incredible wealth. He then turned east, crossed the Hindu Cush Mountains, and went all the way into the Indus Valley, the birthplace of Indian culture. By 540 BC, he had set his sights on conquering Babylon. He defeated the Babylonian armies in a series of battles and opened negotiations for the surrender of King Nabonidus. Camped outside Babylon, Cyrus diverted the Euphrates River into a canal, allowing his men to march into the city during the night through thigh-high water. The city, the king, and the kingdom surrendered (see Dan. 5). Cyrus declared himself "King of Babylon, king of Sumer and Akkad, king of the four corners of the world" (as inscribed on the Cyrus Cylinder).

Tomb of Cyrus the Great, Pasargadae, Iran

In 539 BC, Cyrus made possible the return of Jewish exiles to their homeland. In the Bible, the records of the kings of Israel and Judah conclude with Cyrus's decree:

> The LORD, the God of heaven, has given me all the kingdoms of the earth and he has appointed me to build a temple for him at Jerusalem in Judah. Any of his people among you may go up, and may the LORD their God be with them. (2 Chron. 36:23)

Daniel, the young man who was carried away by Nebuchadnezzar in the first wave of exiles, lived long enough to know that his people were able to return home.

The Cyrus Cylinder

Cyrus Cylinder

In 1879 an archaeologist working for the British Museum discovered a baked clay cylinder buried at the base of an ancient, ruined temple in what had once been the city of Babylon. The cylinder was covered in Akkadian (Babylonian) cuneiform writing and measured about nine inches long with a diameter of about four inches. This cylinder tells part of the story of Cyrus the Great overcoming Babylon, and it provides valuable insight into the religious atmosphere and character of his reign.

In the Old Testament, Cyrus seems sympathetic to the Jewish people and to the Jewish faith. The inscriptions on the cylinder reveal that Cyrus had similar leniency for other faiths as well. This may have been a shrewd political maneuver or a polytheistic tendency—or both.

The writing on the cylinder includes:

- a description of the lapsed faith of the Babylonian ruler Nabonidus,

- a royal genealogy for Cyrus,
- praise for Cyrus's wisdom and reign, and
- a prayer from Cyrus to the Babylonian god Marduk (also called Bel).

The cylinder describes how Cyrus was benevolent toward local worship and "returned gods to their shrines," in contrast with the Babylonians who carried away sacred objects to Babylon. This fits with the biblical narrative which says that under Persian rule temple objects were returned to Jerusalem, and funding to reconstruct the temple was also provided (Ezra 1:7–11). The cylinder is an important archaeological verification of the historical accuracy of the book of Daniel and the Old Testament.

Who was Darius the Mede?

At the end of Daniel 5, we read that "Darius the Mede took over the kingdom, at the age of sixty-two" (verse 31). Then in Daniel 6, we find this same Darius reluctantly giving an order to throw Daniel into the lions' den. The problem is that we don't really know the historical identity of this "Darius the Mede" who was also a king. When the reign of the last Babylonian king, Nabonidus (and his coregent son Belshazzar), came to an end, the reign of Cyrus the Great began. And Cyrus was the conqueror of the city of Babylon. So who was Darius the Mede?

Some scholars suggest that calling him Darius the Mede is simply a mistake by the biblical writers, confusing a later Persian king named Darius with Cyrus, so the book of Daniel cannot be trusted for historical accuracy. Others contend that Daniel 1–6 is a work of fiction, not of actual events. These arguments seem to have a low view of biblical authority and accuracy and fail to take the book of Daniel as it is written and presented.

There are at least two strong possibilities to resolve the identity of Darius the Mede:

(1) Darius may be another name for Cyrus the Great. Cyrus combined the Persian and Median dynasties, and his father was a Persian king and his mother a Median princess. Darius could be a Median name for Cyrus that archaeology has not yet confirmed.

(2) Darius may be another name for the general who first entered and conquered the city of Babylon for Cyrus (Dan. 5:31). Cyrus didn't actually enter the city until days after its capture. A man named Gubaru (also called Ugbaru and Gobryas) had been a Babylonian governor of a region closely connected with Media. Gubaru switched his allegiance from King Nabonidus of Babylonia to King Cyrus of Persia and captured Babylon by surprise. Cyrus gave Gubaru rule of the city of Babylon. So it's possible that Gubaru was considered a type of king who was perhaps called King Darius.

Ultimately, we cannot yet definitively solve the mystery of the identity of Darius the Mede—just as in life some problems seem too complex to unravel. However, we can trust the reliability of the Scriptures and remember that just because we don't have all the answers right now doesn't mean the answers don't exist.

Faithfulness

Faithfulness grows out of faith. Daniel had experienced some of the worst in life. As a young man, he had watched his city burn and was taken away by a foreign king. But Daniel had also experienced some of the best in life. He knew that his friends—Shadrach, Meshach, and Abednego—had been rescued from the fiery furnace when they risked their lives for their faith. He had risen to a position of influence because of his faithful service to the king while maintaining his lifestyle of faithfulness to God.

Through it all, Daniel's confidence in God and in God's promises remained rock solid. He faced a severe test when King Darius banned prayer for thirty days. Wouldn't it have been tempting to skip prayer for a month in order to stay alive? What about praying in a corner or in a secret place or closet—wouldn't that be a way to avoid death while also being faithful? Not for Daniel.

His immediate response was to throw his windows open wide, kneel in plain view, and talk with God. This wasn't a new practice for Daniel simply to provoke a response. It was his customary practice, carried out in persistent, bold faith. Daniel trusted in God, and so he was able to live faithfully. When we trust God's promise, his character, and his presence in our lives, we unlock the potential for faithfulness in every aspect of life: our marriage and family, our career, our gifts and talents, our opportunities, our friendships, and our relationship with God.

> If we follow faithfully only when life is free of trouble, we will value only that trouble-free existence. But if we fasten ourselves to Christ when life is a sinking ship, then we learn to treasure him as our anchor. We discover that our faithfulness is tethered to his, especially during the troubling seasons of life.
>
> GLENNA MARSHALL, *EVERYDAY FAITHFULNESS*

Life Application Questions

1. How did Daniel respond to the king's decree? What does this indicate about Daniel's values and faith?

2. When have you experienced something that seemed like "bad luck" but turned out to be a blessing in disguise?

3. Have there been times when you felt like you were thrown to the lions? What was that experience like? Did you see God working in the midst of it?

4. Daniel's enemies investigated him but could not find any fault in how he conducted his work: "He was neither corrupt nor negligent" (Dan. 6:4). If your enemies investigated how you conduct your work, what would they discover?

5. Daniel's enemies saw that he was the kind of person who would place the law of God above the law of man, and that was the only thing they could convict him of (Dan. 6:5). Is your faith evident enough to "convict" you of being a Jesus-follower?

6. Jealousy drove Daniel's enemies to use manipulative tactics, which ultimately cost them their lives. Examine your heart. What do you need to confess and surrender to God before it damages your life and pollutes your character?

Notes

Daniel 7–9

Daniel's Prayer

Daniel must have longed for freedom and release from exile for his people. Chapter 9 begins with Daniel studying the prophecies of Jeremiah, in which he would have discovered that the Babylonian captivity would last seventy years (Jer. 25:11–12; 29:10). In response to understanding that those seventy years neared completion, Daniel earnestly prays to God.

God's immediate response comes by way of an angelic messenger, Gabriel, who informs Daniel that God's people will continue to suffer until a set time of completion. The "seventy sevens" in Daniel 9:24 seems to be an image that multiplies sevens to indicate divine wholeness, completion, or a designed period of time.

In Daniel's prayer, he describes and appeals to God's character; he takes on the sins of his people and confesses them; and he begs God to intervene and rescue his people.

Read It

Key Bible Passage

Read Daniel 9, which includes Daniel's prayer of intercession for his people and God's response.

Optional Reading

Read Daniel 7–8, which describes visions of world powers and events in the form of four beasts (chapter 7) and a ram and goat (chapter 8).

> We do not make requests of you
> because we are righteous,
> but because of your great mercy.
> DANIEL 9:18

Know It

1. Look again at verses 4–19 in Daniel's prayer.

   - ❑ What does Daniel say about God?

   - ❑ What does Daniel confess?

   - ❑ What does Daniel ask God to do?

2. How does God respond to Daniel's prayer (verses 20–27)?

3. Scripture doesn't tell us what Daniel did or said after God's response. What would you say or do if you were Daniel listening to Gabriel's message from the Lord?

Explore It

Alexander the Great and the Greek Empire

Greek history begins with the Minoan culture on the island of Crete (2600 BC) and the Mycenaean people on the Greek mainland (1400 BC). These early Greeks had some contact with people in the Middle East, as confirmed by Greek pottery found in Canaan. Then, after a thousand years of relative obscurity, Greek culture exploded with the rise of Athens and Sparta (c. 500 BC). Growth in art, literature, philosophy, and architecture, as well as politics and economics, marked this time period.

Athenians and Spartans worked together to fight against a Persian invasion. The Greeks stopped the Persians by winning battles at Marathon and Salamis, including the famous stand of three hundred Spartans against the Persians at the pass of Thermopylae.

Greek unity, however, didn't last. Conflict between Athens and Sparta created an opportunity for Phillip of Macedonia to conquer Greece. Phillip's dream was to unite all of Greece under his reign, and by 338 BC, he had accomplished this goal. But Phillip was unable to enjoy his victory for long. In 336 BC, he was assassinated. It's difficult to know who was responsible, but Phillip's son, Alexander, blamed the Persians.

At the age of twenty, Alexander succeeded his father as king of Macedonia and leader of the Greeks. By the time he was thirty, he had conquered Persia and the ancient world, forming the largest empire in history, stretching from Greece to Egypt and on to India.

Daniel's detailed prophecies about Alexander and the dominance of the Greek Empire—nearly two centuries before Alexander—are startling:

> I saw [the goat] attack the ram furiously, striking the ram and shattering its two horns. The ram was powerless to stand against it; the goat knocked it to the ground and trampled on it, and none could rescue the ram from its power. (Dan. 8:7)
>
> He said: "I am going to tell you what will happen later in the time of wrath, because the vision concerns the appointed time of the end. The two-horned ram that you saw represents the kings of Media and Persia. The shaggy goat is the king of

> Greece, and the large horn between its eyes is the first king." (Dan. 8:19–21)

Alexander pushed east and invaded parts of what is today Afghanistan, Pakistan, and India. His troops, however, refused to cross the formidable Ganges River, so Alexander finally turned back toward home. While in Nebuchadnezzar's former palace in Babylon, Alexander suddenly became ill and died at the age of thirty-three. Once, when asked who should take his place and his empire after his death, Alexander replied, "To the strongest"—setting up forty years of struggle between his top generals.

Alexander's empire was divided between four generals:

- Ptolemy: Egypt and North Africa (Ptolemaic Dynasty)
- Seleucus: East of the Euphrates River to India (Seleucid Dynasty)
- Antigonus: Asia Minor, Syria, and Israel
- Cassander: Greece and Macedonia

Daniel had predicted the four Greek rulers who would follow Alexander:

> The goat became very great, but at the height of its power the large horn was broken off, and in its place four prominent horns grew up toward the four winds of heaven. (Dan. 8:8)

Daniel 11 describes repeated wars between the North (the Seleucids) and the South (the Ptolemies) as well as attempts at peace and alliance through marriage. These two kingdoms carried out a series of battles and peace attempts known in history as the Syrian Wars. For many years, the land of Israel was caught between these two great powers.

The "Little Horn" of Daniel 8

"Out of one of [the four horns] came another horn, which started small but grew in power to the south and to the east and toward the Beautiful Land" (Dan. 8:9). This little horn is believed to be the eighth ruler of the Seleucid Dynasty, Antiochus IV Epiphanes (ruled 175–164 BC). Antiochus and the Seleucids ruled much of the East, including the land of Israel, the Beautiful Land. He took the title Epiphanes for himself, claiming to be an embodiment of the Greek god Zeus. His detractors used a play on words and called him Antiochus Epimanes, which meant "Antiochus the mad."

Antiochus waged war to expand his rule during a time when Rome was a power on the rise. He attacked Cyprus, a holding of the Ptolemies in Egypt. He won victory after victory and pushed King Ptolemy VI into his last stronghold of Alexandria, Egypt. At this point, the Roman Senate intervened to limit Antiochus's reach. He was ordered by a Roman ambassador to withdraw from Egypt and Cyprus, which he did.

Antiochus IV Epiphanes

In Jerusalem, Antiochus had murdered the high priest and installed Menelaus as the new high priest and local ruler. But while Antiochus was campaigning in the South, a false rumor spread in Jerusalem that Antiochus had been killed. The former high priest, Jason, believing the rumor, developed a small army to overthrow Menelaus. Antiochus saw this as an act of rebellion, and he violently attacked the Jews of Jerusalem and Judea. The intertestamental book of 2 Maccabees records what happened next:

> Raging like a wild animal, he set out from Egypt and took Jerusalem by storm. He ordered his soldiers to cut down without mercy those whom they met and to slay those who took refuge in their houses. There was a massacre of young and old, a killing of women and children, a slaughter of young women and infants. In the space of three days, eighty thousand were lost, forty thousand meeting a violent death, and the same number being sold into slavery.

Antiochus was determined to humiliate and subjugate the Jewish people. He made their worship practices and sacrifices illegal, introduced the gods of the Greek pantheon into the temple at Jerusalem, forced priests to eat pork, polluted copies of the Torah, extinguished the temple menorah, and sacrificed a pig on the temple altar. Daniel seems to be describing this time in chapter 8:

> [The little horn] grew until it reached the host of the heavens, and it threw some of the starry host down to the earth and trampled on them. It set itself up to be as great as the commander of the army of the LORD; it took away the daily sacrifice from the LORD, and his sanctuary was thrown down. Because of rebellion, the LORD's people and the daily sacrifice were given over to it. It prospered in everything it did, and truth was thrown to the ground. (Dan. 8:10–12)

In response, the Maccabean Revolt in Judea (167 BC) led to Jewish independence and, for a time, freedom from Seleucid oppression. As for Antiochus, after leaving Jerusalem, he was attacked by Parthians on his eastern border. He never returned from these battles. According to 2 Maccabees, he was struck by God with an intestinal disease, fell from his chariot, and his body was revealed to be consumed with worms while he was still living. He died in agony.

The Statue and the Beasts

Daniel 7 marks the transition in the book of Daniel from narratives about Daniel and his friends to a series of prophetic dreams and visions that God gave to Daniel. In chapter 7, Daniel sees four beasts from the sea. The meaning of this vision is closely connected to that of Nebuchadnezzar's dream of a statue in chapter 2.

NEBUCHADNEZZAR'S DREAM (DAN. 2)	DANIEL'S VISION (DAN. 7)	KINGDOMS
Head of gold	Lion with eagle's wings	Babylonian Empire
Chest and arms of silver	Bear raised on one side; three ribs in its mouth	Medo-Persian Empire
Belly and thighs of bronze	Leopard with four wings and four heads	Greek Empire
Legs of iron and feet of iron and clay	Beast with iron teeth, ten horns; small horn with eyes and a mouth	Roman Empire and the kingdoms that followed
Stone cut out but not by human hands	Son of man coming with the clouds of heaven	Everlasting kingdom of God

The Son of Man

When Daniel begins describing his glimpse into the future, he foresees God (the Ancient of Days) judging all the kingdoms and kings of the earth. He also witnesses God handing the right to rule to someone he calls "a son of man."

> In my vision at night I looked, and there before me was one like a son of man, coming with the clouds of heaven. He approached the Ancient of Days and was led into his presence. He was given authority, glory and sovereign power; all nations and peoples of every language worshiped him. His dominion is an everlasting dominion that will not pass away, and his kingdom is one that will never be destroyed. (Dan. 7:13–14)

The appearance of this son of man is in contrast to the other key actors in Daniel's visions; they appear as beasts and monsters, but the son of man shows up as a human being. However, this "man" is no ordinary person; he rides on clouds, receives all power and authority, and reigns over a divine kingdom that will never end. His common appearance hides the reality of his deity.

Daniel's use of the phrase "son of man" is significant because it becomes an important title for Jesus in the Gospels, in which Jesus frequently refers to himself as the Son of Man. The title is used for Jesus some eighty times in Matthew, Mark, Luke, and John—more than half of which are unique sayings from Jesus not repeated between the Gospels.

In the Gospels, the Son of Man ...

- comes eating and drinking (Matt. 11:19);
- is without a home (Luke 9:58);
- pursues and saves the lost (Luke 19:10);
- will suffer (Mark 8:31);

- gives his life (Mark 10:45) and is betrayed (Luke 22:48);
- possesses heavenly authority (Mark 13:26);
- will return unexpectedly (Luke 12:40) bringing judgment (Luke 17:26–30);
- is joined by angels (Matt. 13:41);
- sits on a throne (Matt. 19:28); and
- is the sacrifice who provides eternal life (John 6:27, 53).

The whole scope of who Jesus is—his personality and character, his deity and humanity, his ministry on earth and ministry in the future—is held within his favorite title for himself: Son of Man.

The prophet Daniel enjoyed the privilege knowing that one would come, claiming the title and authority of the Son of Man. In Jesus, we find the unmatched Son of God who took on humanity to become the Son of Man, claiming the promise of Daniel: "All authority in heaven and on earth has been given to me" (Matt. 28:18).

A Prayer to End Your Day

For around five hundred years, untold numbers of Christians have benefited from following a simple prayer routine first described by Ignatius of Loyola in his guide *Spiritual Exercises*. One of his prayer exercises is designed for the conclusion of the day, usually just before going to sleep. Here are five components to consider for a prayer to end your day:

1. **Ask for light and grace.** Trust yourself to God and enjoy his presence by inviting him to reveal insights about your motivations, attitudes, thoughts, words, and actions. David did this when he prayed, "Search me, God, and know my heart; test me and know my anxious thoughts. See if there is any offensive way in me, and lead me in the way everlasting" (Ps. 139:23–24).

2. **Review your day.** Think through the key events, people, conversations, and actions that made up your day. Hold these significant moments out to God.

3. **Ask forgiveness.** If the Holy Spirit reveals where you fell short in thought, word, or action, confess this failure to God and receive forgiveness. Remember, "if we confess our sins, he is faithful and just and will forgive us our sins and purify us from all unrighteousness" (1 John 1:9).

4. **Celebrate God's presence and gifts.** Look for signs of God's presence throughout your day. How did God send you undeserved gifts? How might God have been protecting or guiding you? Thank God for being with you in every moment!

5. **Commit tomorrow to God.** Today is done and cannot be changed. Tomorrow is a once-in-a-lifetime opportunity to glorify God. Consider what you may experience, and trust every coming moment to the Lord.

Daniel's consistent prayer life shaped his relationship with God. Your consistent prayers over time can shape your heart and life to more closely resemble Jesus.

> Talking to men for God is a great thing, but talking to God for men is greater still. He will never talk well and with real success to men for God who has not learned well how to talk to God for men.
>
> E. M. Bounds, *Power Through Prayer*

Life Application Questions

1. Can anyone make a confessional prayer on behalf of their group—or should a confessional prayer come only from the group's leaders? Consider Daniel's situation when he prayed his confessional prayer.

2. What communities are you part of? Are there any sinful actions that you could confess to the Lord as you represent your community?

3. Does praying regularly come easily for you, or is it difficult to maintain consistent prayer practices? Why?

4. What actions, words, or attitudes have been part of your life recently that you need to confess to the Lord?

5. Remember that forgiveness is always available. Is there anyone or any group of people you need to forgive for wronging you? Is there anyone you need to ask for forgiveness?

6. How would you like to invite God to intervene in your life, the lives of others, your church, your nation, and the world? Use the space below to make a list of your requests.

Notes

Daniel 10–12

A Glimpse into the Future

Is prophecy in the Bible more like a photograph or an impressionist painting?

Take a look at one of your favorite photos. A photograph of a person or place can be very realistic, with intricate detail. Now consider a painting by one of the famous impressionist painters, perhaps *Impression, Sunrise* by Monet or Renoir's *Dance at Le Moulin de la Galette*. Impressionist paintings don't provide the same exacting detail as a photograph, but they do evoke the emotion of a scene and reveal the way shadow, light, and movement give vitality to the natural world and to the people in it. A photograph and a painting both record reality but in their own unique ways.

When we come to prophetic passages in Scripture, we would be wise to remember that, in words, we are viewing a painting more than a photograph. Prophetic literature, like the second half of the book of Daniel, holds powerful meaning for us, but it can be difficult to decipher. Because of this, Christians—even those who agree on the fundamental truths of faith—can have very different interpretations of biblical prophecies.

Read It

Key Bible Passage

Read Daniel 12, God's final message of encouragement to Daniel.

Optional Reading

Read Daniel 10–11, which paints a striking image of conflict in the spiritual world alongside a chaotic world at war.

As for you, go your way till the end. You will rest, and then at the end of the days you will rise to receive your allotted inheritance.

DANIEL 12:13

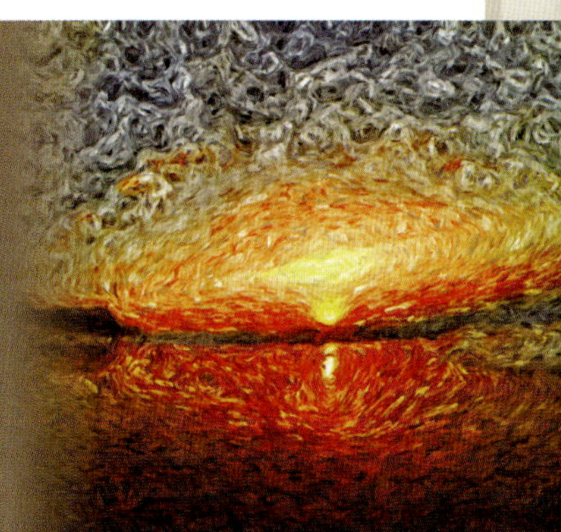

Know It

1. What grabs your attention about the description of the "time of the end" in Daniel 12? What do you have the most questions about?

2. Look again at Daniel 12:1–4. How would you summarize this part of the message?

3. In Daniel 10, how did Daniel react to receiving these prophetic messages from God?

The Three C's of Prophecy

When exploring prophecies in the book of Daniel or elsewhere in the Bible, remember these three words: *cryptic*, *cycles*, and *compressed*.

Cryptic

Prophecy is naturally mysterious. Gospel narratives and New Testament letters are more like photographs than paintings. Stories about Jesus record his actions and teachings; letters from apostles contain specific instructions. Prophets, however, paint in impressionistic colors and cryptic brushstrokes. Their prophecies communicate truth, but it is not easy to discern, and the meaning of any prophecy can be debatable.

Daniel saw visions of future events in the forms of animals, trees, and numbers with hidden meanings. Some of these visions were so strange that they left even the great prophet himself weary and perplexed:

> I, Daniel, was worn out. I lay exhausted for several days. Then I got up and went about the king's business. I was appalled by the vision; it was beyond understanding. (Dan. 8:27)

If Daniel had a hard time understanding his own visions, we too will find prophetic passages difficult to interpret.

Cycles

Prophecy often presents in cycles: repeated failures, repetitions of judgment and repentance, or multiple fulfillments that happen time and again to differing degrees and in different ways. Jeremiah predicted that Babylon would conquer Jerusalem as an act of divine judgment; then Nebuchadnezzar attacked, looted, and devastated the city three times around the sixth century BC. Daniel had visions that "concerned events certain to happen in the future—times of war and great hardship" (Dan. 10:1 NLT). Those "times of war and great hardship" happened in the second century BC when the Seleucid kings, especially Antiochus IV, slaughtered Jews in Judea and defiled their temple. However, those events also happened when the Romans burned the Jerusalem temple in AD 70 and, one could say, much later when the Jewish people were targeted for extermination by Hitler in the Holocaust. It seems likely that the future holds another time of great suffering before Jesus Christ returns at the end of time.

Compressed

Biblical prophecy will often have a near and a far-off fulfillment. Prophets may speak about something that will happen very soon, while also referencing events that could be centuries or even thousands of years in the future without creating a crystal-clear time distinction. This feature can make the prophetic timeline appear compressed. This works hand-in-hand with the idea of cycles. Daniel anticipates events like the rise of the Greek Empire, the conflict between the battling Greek dynasties, and even the rise of Rome, but he also looks ahead to the time of the very end when God will judge all people and reign as king. In the book of Revelation, God makes this compressed aspect of prophecy absolutely clear to John: "Write, therefore, what you have seen, what is now and what will take place later" (Rev. 1:19).

As you study biblical prophecies, it's important to remember that the real power they hold is in the way they strengthen our faith when we fully understand that Jesus the Son of God is the one who will reign forever, make all things new and right, and create blessings for his followers.

The Books of Daniel and Revelation

The book of Revelation and the prophetic chapters in the book of Daniel are known as apocalyptic literature. This is an ancient style of Jewish writing presented in the form of elaborate visions that reveal hidden truths. The word *apocalyptic* comes from the Greek word *apokalypsis*, meaning "unveiling," "unhiding," or "revelation" (hence, the book of Revelation). Bible readers will notice similarities between the visions of Daniel and Revelation; here are just a few:

DANIEL	REVELATION
A little horn waging war against the holy people (Dan. 7:8, 21)	A ten-horned beast waging war against God's holy people (Rev. 13:1, 5–7)
Beasts from the sea that resemble a lion, a bear, and a leopard (Dan. 7:4–6)	A beast from the sea that looks like a leopard with the feet of a bear and a mouth like a lion (Rev. 13:2)
"One like a son of man, coming with the clouds of heaven" (Dan. 7:13)	Seated on a white cloud, "one like a son of man" with a gold crown and a sickle to harvest the earth (Rev. 14:14)
The dead will arise, some to everlasting life and others to everlasting disgrace (Dan. 12:2)	The dead are resurrected and judged, some going to God's dwelling and others to the lake of fire (Rev. 20:12–21:4)

The Roman Empire

The legs of iron along with feet of iron and clay from Nebuchadnezzar's dream in Daniel 2 most likely represent the Roman Empire and the continuing kingdoms of the earth that look back to Rome for inspiration.

While Babylon, Persia, and Greece were rising and falling, a small kingdom in Rome was developing. It had been ruled by kings, then became a republic, before finally entering its imperial era just decades before Jesus was born. By about 146 BC, the Roman Republic represented the greatest military power in the world, and by 49 BC most of Europe and the Middle East was under its authority. The empire was in a state of expansion for decades until reaching the height of its power under Emperor Trajan in AD 117, covering Europe, North Africa, and the Middle East.

The power of Rome was truly like iron, crushing all that came before it. Once the empire finally came to an end in AD 476, successor kingdoms attempted to claim Rome's grandeur and authority. The Byzantine Empire called itself the Eastern Roman Empire and endured until the year 1453 when it was defeated by the Ottomans. In Europe, an empire based in Germany called itself the Holy Roman Empire from the Middle Ages until the early 1800s. Even today, when visiting the capitals of Western nations, remnants of Rome can be discerned in the art and architecture of cities like Washington DC, London, and Paris. In many ways, the powers of the world today seems like a mixture of iron and clay with vestiges of Roman ideals, just as Daniel predicted.

Pont du Gard, Roman aqueduct bridge, France

Resurrection

Daniel 12:1–3 provides one of the clearest teachings in the Old Testament about the resurrection of the dead. The overall focus of the Old Testament is on this life, without extensive teaching about the afterlife. However, several prophets and saints in the Old Testament believed in resurrection and an eternal life to come:

- Abraham believed his son Isaac would be resurrected (Gen. 22:5; Heb. 11:17–19).
- Job affirmed his expectation of physical resurrection (Job 19:25–27).

- David expected to be resurrected (Ps. 16:8–11) and to see his deceased son again (2 Sam. 12:21–23).
- Isaiah taught that the faithful would rise again (Isa. 26:19).

Daniel's description about resurrection joins this tradition of faith. Additionally, Daniel says that all people—believing and unbelieving—will experience *a* resurrection, but their resurrection experiences will be quite different. Some will be raised from the dead to enjoy everlasting life while others will be resurrected to enter "shame and everlasting disgrace" (Dan. 12:2 NLT). This resurrection is often called the general resurrection. The apostle Paul teaches in 1 Corinthians that there will be a physical resurrection of all who have trusted in Jesus and that believers living at the time of Jesus's return will also participate by receiving a new body:

> We will not all sleep, but we will all be changed—in a flash, in the twinkling of an eye, at the last trumpet. For the trumpet will sound, the dead will be raised imperishable, and we will be changed. For the perishable must clothe itself with the imperishable, and the mortal with immortality. (1 Cor. 15:51–53)

After a time that Daniel describes as "anguish" or "distress," faithful believers will be resurrected to eternal life (Dan. 12:1). The apostle John in Revelation builds on Daniel's teaching:

> I saw thrones on which were seated those who had been given authority to judge. And I saw the souls of those who had been beheaded because of their testimony about Jesus and because of the word of God. They had not worshiped the beast or its image and had not received its mark on their foreheads or their hands. They came to life and reigned with Christ a thousand years. (The rest of the dead did not come to life until the thousand years were ended.) This is the first resurrection. Blessed and holy are those who share in the first resurrection. The second death has no power over them, but they will be priests of God and of Christ and will reign with him for a thousand years. (Rev. 20:4–6)

After this thousand-year reign concludes, Satan is released to organize a last rebellion against the reign of God and is defeated. At this final moment, the general resurrection and final judgment follows, in which believers enter everlasting life and unbelievers enter judgment.

Daniel 12 provides part of the foundation for New Testament resurrection concepts, such as those found in Revelation:

> Then I [John] saw a great white throne and him who was seated on it.... I saw the dead, great and small, standing before the throne, and books were opened. Another book was opened, which is the book of life. The dead were judged according to what they had done as recorded in the books. The sea gave up the dead that were in it, and death and Hades gave up the dead that were in them, and each person was judged according to what they had done. Then death and Hades were thrown into the lake of fire. The lake of fire is the second death. Anyone whose name was not found written in the book of life was thrown into the lake of fire. (Rev. 20:11–15)

Revelation 21–22 describe aspects of everlasting life. Resurrection to eternal life is certain for all who have trusted in Jesus. It's rooted in Jesus's own life and resurrection: "I am the resurrection and the life. Anyone who believes in me will live, even after dying. Everyone who lives and believes in me will never die" (John 11:25–26 NLT).

> Jesus laid claim to heavenly dignity and probably to pre-existence itself and claimed to be one who would one day inaugurate the glorious kingdom. But in order to accomplish this, the Son of Man must become the Suffering Servant and submit to death.
>
> **GEORGE ELDON LADD**, *A THEOLOGY OF THE NEW TESTAMENT*

Live It

Faithful to the End

In the twelfth century, a man named Benjamin of Tudela traveled from his home in Spain to the Middle East. His detailed travel journal became an important source of knowledge about the locations and culture of his day.

Tomb of Daniel, Susa, Iran

On one of his stops, he visited Susa, an ancient Persian capital (today in Iran). There, he claimed to have discovered the location of Daniel's tomb. Benjamin recorded an interesting story about how conflict broke out over the final resting place of Daniel's bones, because the community believed the presence of Daniel's remains would bring them prosperity. Eventually, a ruler intervened in the dispute and selected a location as Daniel's resting place where the prosperity could be shared by the largest number of people.

Although no one knows for sure where Daniel's life came to an end, his book and his story end with him in a place similar to where he began: far from home. The young man who had been pulled away from his homeland never returned, but nonetheless, the old man was still living just as faithfully as the young man had. Daniel's life of faith and message forms part of the foundation for our faith. We live far from our eternal home and want to live faithfully like Daniel.

Life Application Questions

1. When you hear the phrase "end times," what comes to mind? How does discussing the end times make you feel?

2. What difference can learning about the end times make in your life, your faith, your perspectives, and your values?

3. Daniel 12:3 says, “Those who are wise shall shine as bright as the sky” (NLT). What does a life of wisdom look like? Give some examples.

4. Verse 3 continues: “Those who lead many to righteousness will shine like the stars forever” (NLT). What might it look like for you to lead someone toward righteousness? Who will you pray for to be brought to righteousness?

5. What are some key things you learned from this study on the book of Daniel?

6. Like Daniel, how can you leave a legacy of faith?

Notes

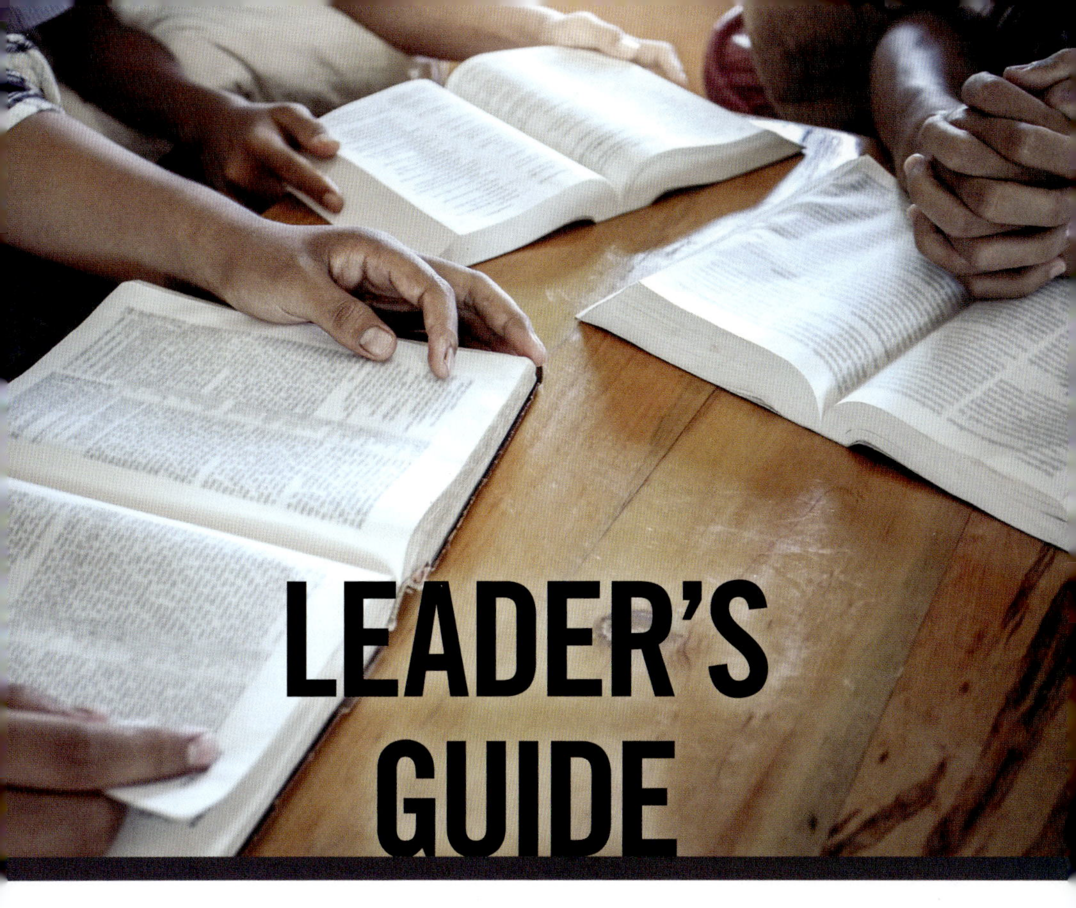

"Encourage one another and build each other up."

1 THESSALONIANS 5:11

Leader's Guide

Congratulations! You've either decided to lead a Bible study, or you're thinking hard about it. Guess what? God does big things through small groups. When his people gather together, open his Word, and invite his Spirit to work, their lives are changed!

Do you feel intimidated yet?

Be comforted by this: even the great apostle Paul felt "in over his head" at times. When he went to Corinth to help people grasp God's truth, he admitted he was overwhelmed: "I came to you in weakness with great fear and trembling" (1 Corinthians 2:3). Later he wondered, "Who is adequate for such a task as this?" (2 Corinthians 2:16 NLT).

Feelings of inadequacy are normal; every leader has them. What's more, they're actually healthy. They keep us dependent on the Lord. It is in our times of greatest weakness that God works most powerfully. The Lord assured Paul, "My grace is sufficient for you, for my power is made perfect in weakness" (2 Corinthians 12:9).

The Goal

What is the goal of a Bible study group? Listen as the apostle Paul speaks to Christians:

- "Oh, my dear children! I feel as if I'm going through labor pains for you again, and they will continue until *Christ is fully developed in your lives*" (Galatians 4:19 NLT, emphasis added).
- "For God knew his people in advance, and he chose them *to become like his Son*" (Romans 8:29 NLT, emphasis added).

Do you see it? God's ultimate goal for us is that we would become like Jesus Christ. This means a Bible study is not about filling our heads with more information. Rather, it is about undergoing transformation. We study and apply God's truth so that it will reshape our hearts and minds, and so that over time, we will become more and more like Jesus.

Paul said, "The purpose of my instruction is that all believers would be filled with love that comes from a pure heart, a clear conscience, and genuine faith" (1 Timothy 1:5 NLT).

This isn't about trying to "master the Bible." No, we're praying that God's Word will master us, and through humble submission to its authority, we'll be changed from the inside out.

Your Role

Many group leaders experience frustration because they confuse their role with God's role. Here's the truth: God alone knows our deep hang-ups and hurts. Only he can save a soul, heal a heart, fix a life. It is God who rescues people from depression, addictions, bitterness, guilt, and shame. We Bible study leaders need to realize that *we can't do any of those things.*

So what can we do? More than we think!

- We can pray.
- We can trust God to work powerfully.
- We can obey the Spirit's promptings.
- We can prepare for group gatherings.
- We can keep showing up faithfully.

With group members:

- We can invite, remind, encourage, and love.
- We can ask good questions and then listen attentively.
- We can gently speak tough truths.
- We can celebrate with those who are happy and weep with those who are sad.
- We can call and text and let them know we've got their back.

But we can never do the things that only the Almighty can do.

- We can't play the Holy Spirit in another person's life.
- We can't be in charge of outcomes.
- We can't force God to work according to our timetables.

And one more important reminder: besides God's role and our role, group members also have a key role to play in this process. If they don't show up, prepare, or open their hearts to God's transforming truth, no life change will take place. We're not called to manipulate or shame, pressure or arm twist. We're not to blame if members don't make progress—and we don't get the credit when they do. We're mere instruments in the hands of God.

> "I planted the seed, [another] watered it, but God has been making it grow. So neither the one who plants nor the one who waters is anything, but only God, who makes things grow."
>
> 1 CORINTHIANS 3:6–7

Leader Myths and Truths

Many people assume that a Bible study leader should:

- Be a Bible scholar.
- Be a dynamic communicator.
- Have a big, fancy house to meet in.
- Have it all together—no doubts, bad habits, or struggles.

These are myths—even outright lies of the enemy!

Here's the truth:

- God is looking for humble Bible students, not scholars.
- You're not signing up to give lectures, you're agreeing to facilitate discussions.
- You don't need a palace, just a place where you can have uninterrupted discussions. (Perhaps one of your group members will agree to host your study.)
- Nobody has it all together. We are all in process. We are all seeking to work out "our salvation with fear and trembling" (Philippians 2:12).

As long as your desire is that Jesus be Lord of your life, God will use you!

Some Bad Reasons to Lead a Group

- You want to wow others with your biblical knowledge.

  "Love . . . does not boast, it is not proud" (1 Corinthians 13:4).

- You're seeking a hidden personal gain or profit.

  "We do not peddle the word of God for profit" (2 Corinthians 2:17).

- You want to tell people how wrong they are.

  "Do not condemn" (Romans 2:1).

- You want to fix or rescue people.

  "It is God who works in you to will and to act" (Philippians 2:13).

- You're being pressured to do it.

  "Am I now trying to win the approval of human beings, or of God?" (Galatians 1:10).

A Few Do's

✔ Pray for your group.

Are you praying for your group members regularly? It is the most important thing a leader can do for his or her group.

✔ Ask for help.

If you're new at leading, spend time with an experienced group leader and pick his or her brain.

✔ Encourage members to prepare.

Challenge participants to read the Bible passages and the material in their study guides, and to answer and reflect on the study questions during the week prior to meeting.

✔ Discuss the group guidelines.

Go over important guidelines with your group at the first session, and again as needed if new members join the group in later sessions. See the *Group Guidelines* at the end of this leader's guide.

✔ Share the load.

Don't be a one-person show. Ask for volunteers. Let group members host the meeting, arrange for snacks, plan socials, lead group prayer times, and so forth. The old saying is true: Participants become boosters; spectators become critics.

✔ Be flexible.

If a group member shows up in crisis, it is okay to stop and take time to surround the hurting brother or sister with love. Provide a safe place for sharing. Listen and pray for his or her needs.

✔ Be kind.

Remember, there's a story—often a heart-breaking one—behind every face. This doesn't *excuse* bad or disruptive behavior on the part of group members, but it might *explain* it.

A Few Don'ts

✘ Don't "wing it."

Although these sessions are designed to require minimum preparation, read each one ahead of time. Highlight the questions you feel are especially important for your group to spend time on.

✘ Don't feel ashamed to say, "I don't know."

Disciple means "learner," not "know-it-all."

✘ Don't feel the need to "dump the truck."

You don't have to say everything you know. There is always next week. A little silence during group discussion time, that's fine. Let members wrestle with questions.

✘ Don't put members on the spot.

Invite others to share and pray, but don't pressure them. Give everyone an opportunity to participate. People will open up on their own time as they learn to trust the group.

✘ Don't go down "rabbit trails."

Be careful not to let one person dominate the time or for the discussion to go down the gossip road. At the same time, don't short-circuit those occasions when the Holy Spirit is working in your group members' lives and therefore they *need* to share a lot.

✘ Don't feel pressure to cover every question.

Better to have a robust discussion of four questions than a superficial conversation of ten.

✘ Don't go long.

Encourage good discussion, but don't be afraid to "rope 'em back in" when needed. Start and end on time. If you do this from the beginning, you'll avoid the tendency of group members to arrive later and later as the season goes on.

How to Use This Study Guide

Many group members have busy lives—dealing with long work hours, childcare, and a host of other obligations. These sessions are designed to be as simple and straightforward as possible to fit into a busy schedule. Nevertheless, encourage group members to set aside some time during the week (even if it's only a little) to pray, read the key Bible passage, and respond to questions in this study guide. This will make the group discussion and experience much more rewarding for everyone.

Each session contains four parts.

Read It

The *Key Bible Passage* is the portion of Scripture everyone should read during the week before the group meeting. The group can read it together at the beginning of the session as well.

The *Optional Reading* is for those who want to dig deeper and read lengthier Bible passages on their own during the week.

Know It

This section encourages participants to reflect on the Bible passage they've just read. Here, the goal is to interact with the biblical text and grasp what it says. (We'll get into practical application later.)

Explore It

Here group members can find background information with charts and visuals to help them understand the Bible passage and the topic more deeply. They'll move beyond the text itself and see how it connects to other parts of Scripture and the historical and cultural context.

Live It

Finally, participants will examine how God's Word connects to their lives. There are application questions for group discussion or personal reflection, practical ideas to apply what they've learned from God's Word, and a closing thought and/or prayer. (Remember, you don't have to cover all the questions or everything in this section during group time. Focus on what's most important for your group.)

Celebrate!

Here's an idea: Have a plan for celebrating your time together after the last session of this Bible study. Do something special after your gathering time, or plan a separate celebration for another time and place. Maybe someone in your group has the gift of hospitality—let them use their gifting and organize the celebration.

	30-MINUTE SESSION	60-MINUTE SESSION
READ IT	Open in prayer and read the *Key Bible Passage.* 5 minutes	Open in prayer and read the *Key Bible Passage.* 5 minutes
KNOW IT	Ask: "What stood out to you from this Bible passage?" 5 minutes	Ask: "What stood out to you from this Bible passage?" 5 minutes
EXPLORE IT	Encourage group members to read this section on their own, but don't spend group time on it. Move on to the life application questions.	Ask: "What did you find new or helpful in the *Explore It* section? What do you still have questions about?" 10 minutes
LIVE IT	Members voluntarily share their answers to 3 or 4 of the life application questions. 15 minutes	Members voluntarily share their answers to the life application questions. 25 minutes
PRAYER & CLOSING	Conclude with a brief prayer. 5 minutes	Share prayer requests and praise reports. Encourage the group to pray for each other in the coming week. Conclude with a brief prayer. 15 minutes

	90-MINUTE SESSION
	Open in prayer and read the *Key Bible Passage.* 5 minutes
	• Ask: "What stood out to you from this Bible passage?" • Then go over the *Know It* questions as a group. 10 minutes
	• Ask: "What did you find new or helpful in the *Explore It* section? What do you still have questions about?" • Here, the leader can add information found while preparing for the session. • If there are questions or a worksheet in this section, go over those as a group. 20 minutes
	• Members voluntarily share their answers to the life application questions. • Wrap up this time with a closing thought or suggestions for how to put into practice in the coming week what was just learned from God's Word. 30 minutes
	• Share prayer requests and praise reports. • Members voluntarily pray during group time about the requests and praises shared. • Encourage the group to pray for each other in the coming week. 25 minutes

Group Guidelines

This group is about discovering God's truth, supporting each other, and finding growth in our new life in Christ. To reach these goals, a group needs a few simple guidelines that everyone should follow for the group to stay healthy and for trust to develop.

1. **Everyone agrees to make group time a priority.**
   We understand that there are work, health, and family issues that come up. So if there is an emergency or schedule conflict that cannot be avoided, be sure to let someone know that you can't make it that week. This may seem like a small thing, but it makes a big difference to your other group members.

2. **What is said in the group stays in the group.**
   Accept it now: we are going to share some personal things. Therefore, the group must be a safe and confidential place to share.

3. **Don't be judgmental, even if you strongly disagree.**
   Listen first, and contribute your perspective only as needed. Remember, you don't fully know someone else's story. Take this advice from James: "Be quick to listen, slow to speak, and slow to become angry" (James 1:19).

4. **Be patient with one another.**
   We are all in process, and some of us are hurting and struggling more than others. Don't expect bad habits or attitudes to disappear overnight.

5. **Everyone participates.**
   It may take time to learn how to share, but as you develop a trust toward the other group members, take the chance.

If you struggle in any of these areas, ask God's help for growth, and ask the group to help hold you accountable. Remember, you're all growing together.

Notes

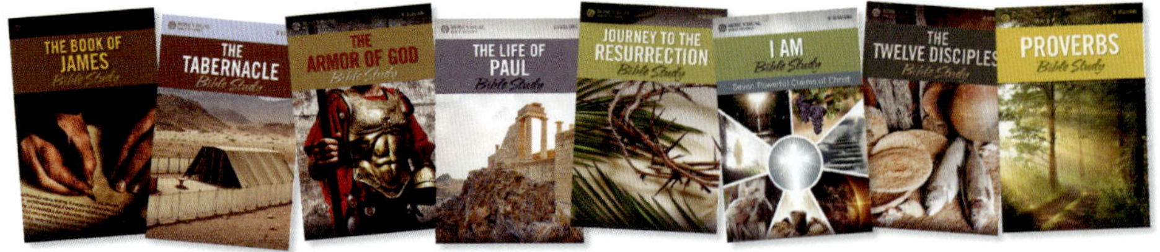

ROSE VISUAL BIBLE STUDIES

6-Session Study Guides for Personal or Group Use

THE BOOK OF JAMES
Find out how to cultivate a living faith through six tests of faith.

THE TABERNACLE
Discover how each item of the tabernacle foreshadowed Jesus.

THE ARMOR OF GOD
Dig deep into Ephesians 6 and learn the meaning of each piece of the armor.

THE LIFE OF PAUL
See how the apostle Paul persevered through trials and proclaimed the gospel.

JOURNEY TO THE RESURRECTION
Renew your heart and mind as you engage in spiritual practices. Perfect for Easter.

I AM
Know the seven powerful claims of Christ from the gospel of John.

THE TWELVE DISCIPLES
Learn about the twelve men Jesus chose to be his disciples.

PARABLES OF JESUS
Understand the key parables of Jesus.

PROVERBS
Gain practical, godly wisdom from the book of Proverbs.

WOMEN OF THE BIBLE: OLD TESTAMENT
Journey through six inspiring stories of women of courage and wisdom.

WOMEN OF THE BIBLE: NEW TESTAMENT
See women's impact in the ministry of Jesus and the early church.

THE LORD'S PRAYER
Deepen your prayer life with the seven petitions in the Lord's Prayer.

FRUIT OF THE SPIRIT
Explore the nine spiritual fruits.

PSALMS
Discover the wild beauty of praise.

THE EXODUS
Witness God's mighty acts in the exodus.

THE BOOK OF JOB
Explore questions about faith and suffering.

THE BOOK OF DANIEL
Be inspired through the stories and prophecies of Daniel.

rose-publishing.com